Argyll and the Islands

A Landscape Fashioned by Geology

Scottish Natural Heritage
Dualchas Nàdair na h-Alba

All of nature for all of Scotland
Nàdar air fad airson Alba air fad

www.snh.gov.uk

© Scottish Natural Heritage 2010

Acknowledgments
Authors: David Stephenson (British Geological Survey) and
Jon Merritt (British Geological Survey)
Series editor: Alan McKirdy (SNH)
Production manager: Pam Malcolm (SNH)
Design and production: SNH Publishing

Photography: David Bell/Ecos 8&9; **Mark Boulton/Alamy** 19 top right;
Laurie Campbell/SNH 14&15; **Peter Cairns/Northshots** 38 left;
Peter Cairns/Wild Wonders of Europe 38 right; **A. Finlayson/BGS** 35;
Lorne Gill/SNH front cover, back cover, frontispiece, 7, 10 left, 10&11,
16&17, 18&19, 20&21, 22&23, 24&25, 26&27, 30&31, 43, 44&45, 46&47,
48 left, 50 top, 50 bottom, 50&51, 52&53, 54&55, 57, 58, 59;
Chris Gomersall/Alamy 50&51; **K. M. Goodenough/SNH** 17 top;
John Gordon 34; **Katia & Maurice Krafft** 19 top left; **Pat & Angus
Macdonald** 4&5, 12&13, 44 left, 49, 56; **Pat & Angus Macdonald/SNH**
opposite contents, 28&29, 41, 54 left; **Fergus MacTaggart** 33;
Iain Thornber 30 left, 36&37; **D. Wolf/Alamy** 48 right.

Illustrations: Richard Bonson 6; **Craig Ellery** 2, 3, 22, 39, 42;
Iain McIntosh 1.

ISBN: 978 1 85397 608 7

Print Code SP1.5K0910

Further copies are available from: Publications,
Scottish Natural Heritage, Battleby, Redgorton, Perth PH1 3EW
Tel 01738 458530 Fax 01738 456613 pubs@snh.gov.uk

Front cover image and Frontispiece:
View north over the rocky shore and
raised beach at Port Appin towards
Loch Linnhe.
Back cover image:
Conglomerate of the Old Red
Sandstone at Gylen Castle, Kerrera.

Argyll and the Islands

A Landscape Fashioned by Geology

by

David Stephenson and Jon Merritt

1

Contents

1
The Isle of Oronsay, in the foreground, is separated from the larger Isle of Colonsay by the tidal flats known as The Strand, which can be driven across at low tide. Falling sea levels since the last ice age have made this possible.

Introduction

Between the 5th and 9th centuries AD, the peninsulas and islands of western Argyll, together with Arran and the coastal areas of Antrim, formed the ancient Scots' kingdom of Dalriada. Stand on a prominent hill anywhere in the area on a clear day and it is easy to appreciate just how this coastal kingdom functioned. The islands and headlands are all visible from each other, making navigation by sea the most practicable option. The inland areas were, and still are, a different matter. The hills are not as high as elsewhere in the Highlands but this is probably some of the roughest terrain in Scotland, with steep boulder-strewn ridges separated by boggy vegetated valleys that severely restrict cross-country movement even to this day.

Why should it be like that? What is it that controls the long ridges and the coastline, with its series of parallel sea lochs, unique in the British Isles? The answer lies in the 700 to 550 million year-old bedrock, consisting of layers of rock with highly varied resistance to erosion. These have been folded and reorientated by the great 'Caledonian' earth movements some 470 million years ago, so that their outcrops run consistently southwest to northeast. Throughout the Grampian Highlands those rocks are known as the 'Dalradian', in honour of the ancient kingdom.

Locally there are younger rocks; volcanic lavas, sandstones and even coal measures. But the landscape details that we see today are mainly the result of deep scouring by glaciers that finally melted here around 11,500 years ago and of the effects of subsequent changes in sea level.

1
Paps of Jura from Ballochroy.

Argyll and the Islands Through Time

QUATERNARY
2.6 million years ago to the present day

11,500 years ago to the present day. The climate warmed abruptly and our present 'Interglacial' period began. Dense woodland was present by 8,000 years ago, and sea level peaked at about 12m above present-day levels at about 6,500 years ago, before dropping again.

12,600 to 11,500 years ago. Full glacial conditions returned and outlet glaciers readvanced into the sea from the mountains to the east.

14,700 to 12,600 years ago. A period of warmer climate, much like that of today, led to the rapid melting of the glaciers. Sea level was much higher than today, but falling rapidly

29,000 to 14,700 years ago. A thick ice sheet covered the whole of Scotland for the last time, extending to the continental shelf margin, with only the highest peaks protruding through the ice.

Before 29,000 years ago. Numerous prolonged, very cold periods were interspersed with shorter, warmer episodes. Widespread glaciations affected the region on at least two occasions.

NEOGENE
23 to 2.6 million years ago

The high ground of the western Highlands was gradually eroded under subtropical and then warm, temperate conditions, cooling gradually until 2.6 million years ago when the Ice Age began.

PALAEOGENE
65 to 23 million years ago

About 60 million years ago, volcanoes erupted to the west of the Highlands, eventually leading to the opening of the North Atlantic Ocean. Magma was intruded across Argyll as NW-trending dykes.

CRETACEOUS
145 to 65 million years ago

Warm, shallow seas covered most of Scotland, which was now around 45 degrees north, but higher parts of the Highlands might have remained above sea level.

JURASSIC
200 to 145 million years ago

The area that is now the Scottish Highlands formed high ground on the margins of shallow seas, and dinosaurs roamed along the coast.

TRIASSIC
251 to 200 million years ago

Seasonal rivers flowed westwards across open plains depositing wide spreads of silts, sands and pebbly gravels.

PERMIAN
299 to 251 million years ago

Scotland had drifted 10 to 20 degrees north of the equator and was again hot and dry, with desert sands accumulating on lower ground.

CARBONIFEROUS
359 to 299 million years ago

Scotland lay close to the equator. Low-lying plains with tropical forests covered central Scotland and extended over parts of the Highlands. Volcanoes erupted on the Mull of Kintyre and coal was formed around Machrihanish.

DEVONIAN
416 to 359 million years ago

Scotland had become part of a vast, arid continent. Rivers washed debris onto flood plains and into lakes to form the Old Red Sandstone.

SILURIAN
444 to 416 million years ago

The Argyll area lay about 15 degrees south of the Equator. It was dry and mountainous, with deep valleys that flooded during rare wet periods. Magma accumulated at depth, and cooled to form granites. It also rose up through the crust and erupted at the surface to form the Lorn volcanoes.

ORDOVICIAN
488 to 444 million years ago

Colliding continents formed the Caledonian mountain chain; the Dalradian sediments were buried, compressed and heated, and deformed into spectacular folds.

CAMBRIAN
542 to 488 million years ago

Sediments, now best seen in the North-west Highlands, were deposited on the flanks of Laurentia, whilst other continental masses moved ever closer together, narrowing the intervening ocean.

PRECAMBRIAN
Before 542 million years ago

600 million years ago, Rodinia was split by the development of a new ocean called Iapetus; sub-marine volcanoes erupted and Dalradian sediments continued to be deposited on the edge of a new continent called Laurentia. **Starting about 730 million years ago,** the Dalradian sediments were laid down on the edge of a continent known as Rodinia. **Around 1800 million years ago,** new magma was injected into the Earth's crust and was transformed into the gneisses of the Rhinns of Islay.

Brown bars indicate periods of time represented by the rocks and loose sediments seen in the Argyll area.

Geological Map of Argyll and the Islands

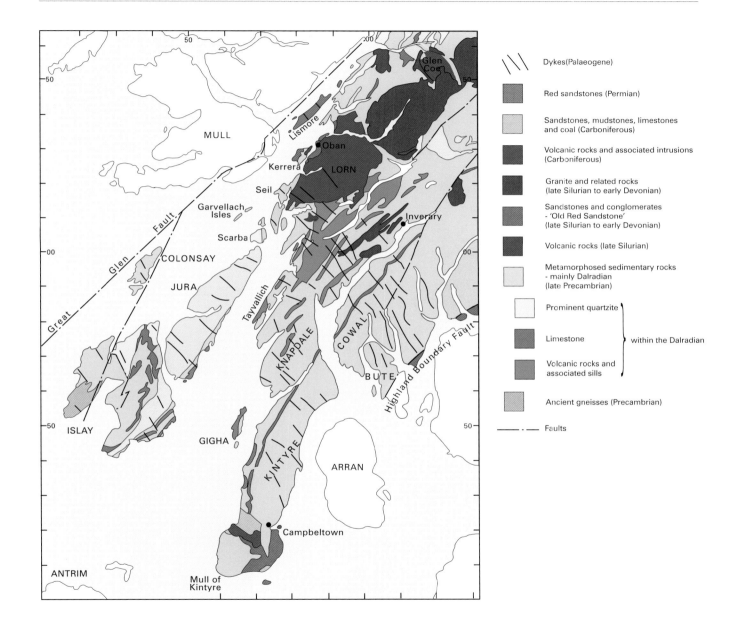

Legend:

- Dykes (Palaeogene)
- Red sandstones (Permian)
- Sandstones, mudstones, limestones and coal (Carboniferous)
- Volcanic rocks and associated intrusions (Carboniferous)
- Granite and related rocks (late Silurian to early Devonian)
- Sandstones and conglomerates - 'Old Red Sandstone' (late Silurian to early Devonian)
- Volcanic rocks (late Silurian)
- Metamorphosed sedimentary rocks - mainly Dalradian (late Precambrian)
- Prominent quartzite ⎫
- Limestone ⎬ within the Dalradian
- Volcanic rocks and associated sills ⎭
- Ancient gneisses (Precambrian)
- — · — Faults

Map labels:

MULL, Lismore, Oban, Kerrera, LORN, Glen Coe, Seil, Inverary, Garvellach Isles, Scarba, COLONSAY, JURA, Tayvallich, KNAPDALE, COWAL, BUTE, Highland Boundary Fault, Great Glen Fault, ISLAY, GIGHA, KINTYRE, ARRAN, Campbeltown, Mull of Kintyre, ANTRIM

In the Beginning: the Birth of the Caledonian Mountains

The Scottish Highlands are just part of an ancient mountain range, comparable to the present day Alps or Himalayas, which was once over five thousand kilometres long. Today its eroded remnants are found in eastern North America, east Greenland, Ireland, Scotland and Norway, separated by the much younger North Atlantic Ocean. Throughout their length these are known as the Caledonian Mountains and the series of powerful earth movements that formed them is known as the Caledonian Orogeny.

The rocks that underlie most of the Highlands and Islands southeast of the Great Glen are known as the Dalradian. Most originated as sediment laid down between 730 and 600 million years ago in and around shallow seas on an ancient continent known as Rodinia. About 600 million years ago, this continent was pulled apart by slow movements of the huge tectonic plates that form the outer layer of the Earth. Some of the evidence for this continental break-up is found in Argyll, where there are great thicknesses of volcanic rocks that erupted beneath a developing ocean called the Iapetus Ocean. The foundations of Scotland were on the edge of this new ocean and, together with North America and Greenland, they broke away to became part of a new continent, which we refer to as Laurentia. Sediment then continued to be laid down on the margin of Laurentia for almost the next 100 million years.

1

The coast-parallel sea lochs and islands of peninsula Argyll, seen here at Loch Craignish, are unique in the British Isles.

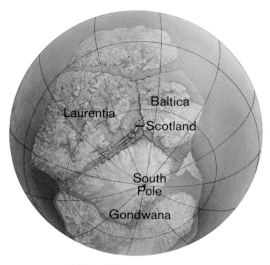

600 million years ago

A supercontinent called Rodinia, situated around the South Pole, starts to break up into individual tectonic plates, leaving Scotland on the edge of a new continent called Laurentia that also includes North America and Greenland.

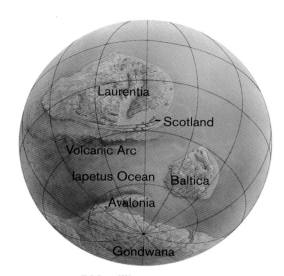

500 million years ago

An ocean called Iapetus now separates Laurentia from the continents of Avalonia (including England and Wales) and Baltica (including Norway, Sweden and Finland). Slowly the continents converge and the ocean closes.

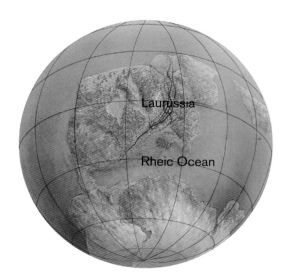

400 million years ago

Closure of the Iapetus Ocean is complete. Baltica has collided 'head on' with Laurentia whereas Avalonia has 'docked' more gently to the south. Scotland now lies in the arid zone south of the equator, close to the centre of a continent called Laurussia.

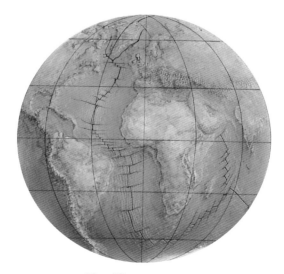

40 million years ago

The North Atlantic Ocean opens 80 million years ago and, at 55 million years, Greenland splits off from Europe. North America and Europe continue to drift apart to this day.

2

Laurentia was separated by the Iapetus Ocean from the continent of Baltica (the foundations of Sweden, Finland and Russia) and from a smaller continent called Avalonia, on which the rocks of England and Wales were forming. But, some 500 million years ago, tectonic forces started to move the three continents closer together and gradually the ocean closed up. The rocks in front of the moving continents crumpled and folded, just as a tablecloth does when you slide it across a tabletop, and eventually, by about 430 million years ago, the continents collided and became welded together. By this process the Earth's crust along the weld became very much thicker than normal. The rocks that were deeply buried were heated and recrystallised, growing new minerals in the process that we know as metamorphism. In extreme cases, the rocks melted to form magma, which accumulated in vast magma chambers, deep below the surface. Continental crust is less dense than the Earth's interior and hence it is buoyant and slowly rises. Crust that has been thickened rises higher than normal crust, just as a large iceberg rises to a greater height above sea level than a smaller iceberg, and hence mountain ranges are formed; the Himalayas are still rising today at a rate of between 1 and 4 millimetres a year.

2
Black slaty mudstones and a bed of pale limestone on Kerrera have been folded during the 'Caledonian' earth movement some 470 million years ago.

The Oldest Rocks

The oldest rocks in the region are in the west, where they form the southern part of the Rhinns of Islay. They are around 1,800 million years old, much older than the Dalradian rocks, but not as old as the oldest rocks on the British Isles, the Lewisian gneisses of the Outer Hebrides and North-west Highlands. The rocks of the Rhinns are also gneisses; they are coarsely crystalline and have a strongly banded appearance with pale and dark layers. It is thought that they formed when new material was being added to the Earth's crust by the injection of molten material (magma) from deep within the Earth. The landscape is distinctly different from anywhere else in the region and consists of rounded rocky knolls separated by flat bottomed valleys and peaty hollows. In fact, it looks more like the Outer Hebrides than the Grampian Highlands.

The rocks that overlie the gneisses form the north of the Rhinns and the islands of Oronsay and Colonsay. Geologists have argued about the age and affinities of these rocks for many years but they look very similar to the Dalradian rocks and are most likely to be related. Landscapes in these areas are comparable to those of Dalradian outcrops elsewhere on the exposed western seaboard of the region.

1

The pink gneisses of the Rhinns of Islay, seen here at Lossit Point, are the oldest rocks of the region. The landscape is more like the Outer Hebrides than Argyll.

1

Caledonian Foundations: the Dalradian Rocks

The geological foundations of the southwestern Highlands are mainly the Dalradian rocks. These were deposited 730 to 500 million years ago as sands, muds and limy deposits in shallow seas, on coastal plains and on the margins of an ocean. As these sediments were buried and compressed, they became sandstones, mudstones and limestones. During the Caledonian earth movements, 470 to 430 million years ago, these rocks were subjected to much greater stresses and high temperatures. The original sediment grains were recrystallised into new minerals and many of the rocks developed a new layering that reflected the crushing forces around them. Mudstones became schists and slates; sandstones became very hard, cream-to-white quartzites, and some of the limestones became beautifully patterned marbles. At the end of the orogeny these rocks were uplifted to form the young Caledonian Mountains.

Over millions of years, the Caledonian Mountains have been worn down and carved into the hills that we see today. The slates and schists provide few distinctive natural landscape features and tend to form smooth, rounded slopes and hills, well seen on the so-called 'slate islands' of Shuna, Luing and Seil. The slates led to early industrial development in the region and were exported throughout Scotland and to England, Ireland and even to North America at one time. They can be easily distinguished on roofs to this day on account of the cubic crystals, a centimetre or more across, of shiny yellow pyrite (fool's gold) that they contain.

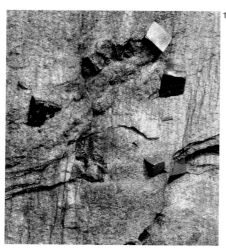

1
Cubes of pyrite (iron sulphide) in the Easdale slate.
2
The pier at Easdale is constructed from the local slate.

Beds of limestone (marble) are particularly notable on Lismore. Apart from some interbedded black slates, virtually the whole island is made of limestone and, consequently, has a landscape that is unique in this part of the Highlands. The well-drained hillsides are covered in short grass, cropped by grazing animals, and are renowned for the wild flowers that thrive on the limy soil.

3
The lush green vegetation of the Isle of Lismore is a result of its limestone and slate bedrock.

It is the quartzites that form the most obvious landscape features. They are formed almost entirely of grains of quartz (silica), which are firmly cemented together, making them very hard and resistant to erosion. They tend to form all of the higher and most obvious peaks and ridges of the region, in particular the Paps of Jura and the mountains of Islay that form such good landmarks. The summits of these mountains are composed of loose blocks of quartzite, shattered by the action of frost during and immediately after the last glaciation. Quartzites are also responsible for many prominent coastal headlands such as the Mull of Oa.

4
Cliffs of quartzite
at the Mull of Oa.

6

Although they do not form distinctive landscape features, there is one group of rocks that has drawn international attention to the Argyll islands. These are the Port Askaig 'boulder beds', which occur in a sequence up to 750 metres thick around Port Askaig on Islay and on the Garvellach Isles.

Essentially these are fossilised glacial deposits, formed initially by the grinding action of debris caught up in the base of an ice sheet. They contain large rounded boulders and some exposures could easily be mistaken for more-recent glacial deposits, except that the boulders are set in solid rock. They are important because they show that a major glacial period occurred some 635 million years ago on the continent of Rodinia, one of several glacial events throughout Earth's history that are helping geologists, glaciologists and climatologists to understand the processes of global climate change.

The most obvious features of the areas around Loch Awe, Knapdale and the southeast coasts of Jura and Islay are parallel outcrops of dark green to black rocks that generally form resistant ridges and headlands, and almost completely enclose sheltered bays in places. These are the products of volcanic activity that accompanied the birth of the Iapetus Ocean, as the continent of Rodinia split apart 600 million years ago. They are known as the Tayvallich volcanic rocks.

5
Ardilistry Bay from Cnoc Rhaonastil. The bays on the southeast coast of Islay are eroded out of relatively soft slates, whereas the headlands are of more resistant metamorphosed igneous rocks.
6
These ancient glacial deposits within the Dalradian rocks of the Garvellach Isles were formed 635 million years ago. Compare them with the photograph of more-recent glacial till on page 35.

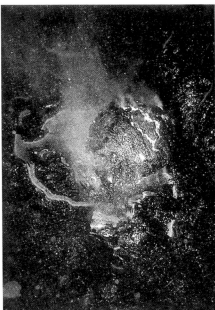

Some rocks formed from basalt lava that erupted on the ocean floor. The lava surface 'froze' immediately as it made contact with the sea water and formed a thin 'skin' of glassy rock around pillow-shaped blobs and tubes of still-molten, still-erupting magma. The magma continually broke through the solid skin and the process was repeated to build up a pile of what are known as 'pillow lavas'. Some remarkable examples are preserved around Tayvallich. Throughout Argyll, much of the magma never reached the surface and solidified at shallow depths in horizontal sheets called 'sills'.

Ironically the rocks that make up the lavas and sills and form resistant landscape features are also very easy to carve. The orientation of new minerals that grew during the Caledonian earth movements enables them to be split into slabs. Consequently they were the preferred material for the construction of the many celtic crosses that are a feature not just of this region and also all along the western seaboards of Scotland and Ireland.

7
Pillow lavas form when magma erupts underwater and chills instantly to form blobs with glassy crusts. These ones at Tayvallich are 600 million years old.
8
Modern pillow lavas erupting on the sea bed around Kilauea, Hawaii.
9
Some of the igneous rocks are very easily carved and were in great demand in medieval times for Celtic crosses, grave slabs and other monuments such as Kildalton High Cross, Islay.

The First Caledonian Mountains and the 'Old Red Sandstone'

The uplift of the Earth's crust towards the end of the Caledonian Orogeny left a range of high mountains with steep unstable slopes, separated by deep valleys and some broader basins with lakes and flood plains. The climate was generally hot and dry, and at that point in Earth's history, some 425 million years ago, there was hardly any vegetation. So, when it did rain there was nothing to hold back the run-off, and dramatic flash floods carrying vast amounts of rock debris were the norm.

The products of those floods are spectacularly displayed in many road cuttings around Oban and Benderloch. Huge rounded boulders, some over a metre across, are embedded in a hard gritty matrix to form thick deposits of the rock type known as 'conglomerate'. The conglomerates are mostly buried beneath a thick sequence of lava flows, although episodes of flooding between volcanic eruptions left further conglomerates between the flows. On the island of Kerrera, conglomerate can be seen resting upon upturned beds of Dalradian rock that formed the bedrock of the Caledonian Mountains. The irregular junction between the two rock types is the pre-flood land surface, and, represents a gap in the geological record of some 200 million years. Geologists call these surfaces and time gaps 'unconformities'.

More extensive outcrops of conglomerate, interbedded with purplish red and white sandstones and some mudstones, form the rounded hills south of Campbeltown and on Sanda Island. Here, wider valleys and basins were gradually being filled by finer grained sediments, deposited from rivers flowing out of the mountains onto the plains at their foot.

1
These spectacular conglomerates on Kerrera are the product of flash floods in a dry mountain area some 420 million years ago.

2

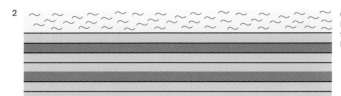

630 million years ago: muds were laid down on sea-bed and hardened to form layers of mudstone and limestone.

470 million years ago: rocks were folded deep in the Earth's crust.

430 million years ago: rocks were uplifted to the surface and eroded by rivers that deposited sand and gravel on top of the folded rocks.

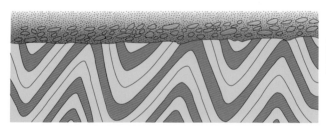

lava
sandstone
conglomerate
UNCONFORMITY

Dalradian

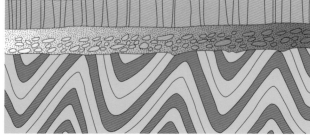

425 million years ago: volcanoes erupted lava that buried the sand and gravel.

2
Diagram showing the unconformity on Kerrera
3
The unconformity on Kerrera clearly shows 420 million-year-old conglomerates resting upon tightly folded 620 million-year-old slates.

Tropical Swamps and Deserts: the Carboniferous and Permian Periods

The extensive low-lying and flat ground to the north and east of Machrihanish is underlain by the Machrihanish Coalfield. An 800 metre-thick sequence of Carboniferous-age sandstone, siltstone, mudstone and limestone has been proved in boreholes and mine workings, but hardly any bedrock is exposed as it is covered by relatively recent raised beach deposits, alluvium and blown sand. The sandstones and siltstones formed some 330 to 300 million years ago on wide coastal plains that were periodically inundated by the sea, in which the limestone formed. Trees that grew in tropical forests fell into oxygen-starved swamps where, instead of rotting, they were compressed to form coal.

Coal seams up to 3 metres thick have been worked intermittently at Machrihanish since the end of the 18th century, but the last mine closed in 1967 after a serious fire. The sequence of rocks is very similar to that found in the coalfields of central Scotland. Its presence in the Highlands is due to a block of the Earth's crust that has dropped down between two northwest-trending fractures ('faults'), bringing a cover of younger sedimentary rocks down to the same level as the older Dalradian rocks. The sedimentary rocks were much more easily worn away than the surrounding Dalradian rocks, and hence the area of the coalfield rarely exceeds 20 metres above sea level.

A further very small outcrop of Carboniferous-age sandstones and mudstones, also associated with a northwest-trending fault, is found in the River Awe at the Pass of Brander. Together, these outcrops demonstrate that tropical shallow seas, lowland forests and coal-forming swamps extended, at least locally, from the Scottish lowlands across the Highland Boundary in Carboniferous times.

1

The low-lying ground between Campbeltown and Machrihanish is underlain by easily eroded coal-bearing sedimentary rocks of Carboniferous age. These are covered by relatively recent raised beach deposits, which provide a wide flat surface for one of the longest airport runways in Europe.

1

In the succeeding Permian times, Scotland lay at a similar latitude to the present-day Sahara Desert, and wind-blown desert sands formed many of the sandstones of this age. They are known to occur offshore in a wide sedimentary basin between Antrim, Kintyre and Islay, but onshore the distinctive bright-red sandstones are seen only along the coast between Bellochantuy and Tayinloan. On small islets in the Sound of Islay they are overlain by basalt lava.

2
Red sandstones of Permian age are seen along the coast between Bellochantuy Bay and Tayinloan.

Three More Ages of Volcanoes

The 600 million-year-old Tayvallich volcanic rocks were just the first of several volcanic episodes to affect the Argyll area. As the first Caledonian mountains were being uplifted, melting of rocks deep within and below the Earth's crust formed magma that accumulated and rose towards the surface. In some cases the magma became trapped, causing it to cool slowly, forming rocks with large crystals up to a few centimetres in size. Granite is a rock that formed in this way, in large bodies many kilometres across, called plutons. The Etive Pluton in northern Argyll is one of the biggest in the Highlands and forms the highest mountains of the region described in this book, such as Ben Starav and Ben Cruachan.

In places the magma was able to rise through fractures all the way to the surface, where it erupted as lava around 425 million years ago. The relatively fluid basalt and andesite lavas spread out over a wide area around Oban, where in many places they can be seen resting horizontally upon conglomerates. Today the lavas form flat-topped moors and stepped hillsides of the area known as the Lorn Plateau. Some of the lavas on Kerrera developed hexagonal columns as they cooled, and they look like smaller versions of those on the Isle of Staffa and the Giant's Causeway.

In the south of Kintyre, the hills to the south and southeast of Machrihanish are composed of lavas that erupted in early Carboniferous time, around 340 million years ago. In places the dominantly basalt lavas form wide terraced hillsides like those of Lorn but some formed from sticky, viscous, more silica-rich lava (trachyte) that was squeezed out as steep-sided domes, preserved as prominent knolls such as Skerry Fell Fad.

1
The high mountains at the head of Loch Etive, including Ben Starav and Ben Cruachan, are carved out of a large mass of granite intruded at the end of the 'Caledonian' earth movements. 1

Later still, around 60 million years ago, huge volcanoes formed in the Inner Hebrides, as fractures spread through the Earth's crust just prior to the formation of the North Atlantic Ocean. Countless northwest to southeast trending fractures extended across Argyll, many seeming to emanate from a central volcano on Mull.

The fractures became filled with magma that solidified to form vertical sheets of rock up to several metres wide called dykes, some of which can be traced as far as the coast of north Yorkshire. They are particularly well seen on the coast, where they either stand proud of softer surrounding rock as walls, or form trenches within harder country rocks.

2
Northwest-trending, 60 million year-old dykes on the west coast of Jura stand proud above the modern-day beach.

3
Skerry Fell Fad, above Machrihanish, is a dome formed from sticky, viscous trachyte lava, within a sequence of dominantly basalt lavas, which erupted some 340 million years ago during Carboniferous time.

Into the Ice Age

After the volcanic eruptions in the Inner Hebrides, the continental crust to the west of Scotland split completely and magma, rising up from deep in the Earth, was erupted to form a new ocean floor. This was the birth of the North Atlantic Ocean, which continues to widen in the same way to this day, with volcanic eruptions along the submerged Mid-Atlantic Ridge and on Iceland. When the volcanic activity ceased in Scotland, the exposed rocks on land were largely decomposed to sand and clay under first warm, and then cooler, humid conditions that lasted until the beginning of the Ice Age.

The Ice Age began when ice sheets first advanced across the Northern Hemisphere, about 2.6 million years ago. Since then, cold 'glacial' periods have been separated by much shorter warmer 'interglacials', when the climate of Scotland was sometimes warmer than at the present day. Evidence of these early glaciations has been largely destroyed by subsequent glacial erosion, but extensive ice sheets covered Argyll and extended out to sea on at least three separate occasions.

The last major glaciation was at its peak about 22,000 years ago, when a vast sheet of ice flowed westwards from an 'ice divide' (the equivalent to a watershed) that stretched between Ben Nevis and Arran. The ice plucked up rocks from the mainland and carried them directly towards Islay and Jura, where some of them were deposited as 'glacial erratics'. The Scottish ice sheet eventually thinned and retreated slowly whilst the climate remained very cold and dry. The flow of ice gradually became constrained by the underlying topography and at this stage many outlet glaciers would have flowed through the sounds and sea lochs of the district, rather like in Greenland and Alaska today. Icebergs calved off these glaciers regularly, bringing about their eventual rapid retreat.

1
The quartzite mountains of the Paps of Jura seen from the Sound of Islay.

The summits of the Paps of Jura emerged relatively early from the ice, and as they became exposed to extreme freezing and thawing conditions, these small mountains were reduced to extraordinary piles of quartzite rubble. A remarkable 3.5 kilometre-long belt of boulders descends northwestwards from one of the paps, Sgiob na Caillich, towards the sea. It formed as two glaciers converged in the lee of the mountain and is perhaps the finest example of a fossil 'medial moraine' in the British Isles.

2
Medial moraine, the Paps of Jura.
3
Glacial till exposed in Glen Lussa, Kintyre.

2

3

The most widespread deposit laid
down directly by glaciers is known
as 'till' or 'boulder clay'. In Argyll it
is mainly confined to pockets within
rock. Till was laid down beneath the
sole of the glacier and consists of
boulders, cobbles and pebbles mixed
with sand and 'rock flour' ground-up
by the flowing ice. Tills represent
some of the least permeable deposits
and consequently commonly underlie
boggy ground. Stones within tills
strongly reflect the nature of the
underlying bedrock from which
they were plucked, but some are
far travelled and provide a clue to
former directions of ice flow during
glaciations.

A False Dawn

A sudden climatic warming occurred 14,700 years ago. The rate of glacial retreat that occurred then was probably even more rapid than it is in the world today. For a thousand years or so, summer temperatures were at least as high as at present and pioneer plant species soon began to colonise the bare, stony soils. Pollen and spores preserved within a silted-up lake near Oban provide an important record of this period of time. Shellfish and other marine organisms flourished in the sea lochs and their remains may be found locally in deposits of shelly silt and clay. A good place to look for these deposits is on the foreshore at South Shian.

However, it was a false dawn, for the climate soon started to cool again and by 12,650 years ago ice was accumulating in the high corries of Skye, Mull and Arran. A large ice sheet formed in the western Highlands from which outlet glaciers flowed towards the sea, entering sea lochs like Loch Fyne. Glaciers reached the mouths of lochs Leven, Etive and Creran, where they formed terminal moraines partly created from the shelly deposits that the ice had bulldozed forward from the loch floors. A splendid suite of terrace features, mounds and ridges that formed at the snout of the Etive glacier may be observed between Connel and Achnaba, at the mouth of the loch.

Beyond the glaciers, the rest of the Argyll district had a dry, Arctic climate similar to the tundra of Siberia and northern Canada today, where freeze-thaw, 'periglacial' processes, such as frost-heaving and frost-shattering, operated. Boulders and soil crept down steep slopes to form distinctive lobes. Screes formed as frost-shattered rocks tumbled down cliffs. Anyone who accepts the challenge of climbing the Paps of Jura will appreciate the power of periglacial processes in reducing hard rocks to rubble. They will also be able to view one of the best examples in Scotland of a fossil 'rock glacier'. This lobate accumulation of quartzite blocks lies at the foot of Beinn Shiantaidh, where it includes several concentric ridge crests and odd, semicircular depressions. Unlike a true glacier formed of ice derived from snowfields, rock glaciers of the type found on Jura formed in a periglacial environment, as ice gradually filled in the voids within rubbly, scree-like deposits. The mass of rock and ice was able to creep very slowly downhill.

1
The quartzites of the Paps of Jura developed a mantle of frost-shattered blocks during glacial times.

After the Ice

The last glacial period halted abruptly about 11,500 years ago when our relatively warm, wet climate dominated by the Gulf Stream began. The profound changes in the landscape and vegetation that ensued have been discovered mainly from studying pollen, insect remains and other microfossils contained within lake sediments at Loch Cill an Aonghais in southern Knapdale, and in intertidal muds and peat bogs elsewhere in the district. A pioneer community of herbaceous plants soon began to colonise the thin, stony soils, followed by a mosaic of heather, juniper and grass. Birch was the first tree to migrate into the area about 9,600 years ago, followed quickly by the arrival of hazel and elm, and then oak from about 8,500 years ago. A dense, temperate rainforest covered most of the district by 6,000 years ago, when the climate had become particularly mild. Man hunted in the forest, which contained many animals that are now extinct, including bears, wolves and beavers. His impact on the environment increased around 5,000 years ago, when he started making small clearings in the forest. This clearance gradually became more extensive whilst the climate became cooler and wetter, peat bogs expanded, and rates of soil erosion increased. Widespread cereal and flax cultivation began in the area about 800 years ago.

1

2

1
European brown bear.
2
European beaver, recently re-introduced
and now breeding again in Argyll.
3
Reconstruction of how the area may
have looked 6,000 years ago.

Ancient Shores and Cliffs

The much indented coastline of Argyll and the islands is characterised by long abandoned platforms cut into the rocks by waves, which have now been raised up to 55 metres above present-day sea level. Indeed, these widespread benches and notches carved into the cliffs add considerably to the splendour and mystery of this rugged coastline, helping to create those iconic views of glorious sunsets over the skerries and islands to the west. Several distinct sets of features occur that have formed at different times, and they are best developed on the northwest coast of Jura and northern Islay.

The higher platforms were fashioned at various times over the past half a million years or so, during several major glaciations. They are partially concealed beneath glacial deposits and have been scratched and polished by ice locally. Platforms lying between about 40 metres and 10 metres above present sea level formed mostly towards the end of the last glaciation, some 15,000 years ago. They are commonly capped by shingle in 'raised beaches' that formed when the vast quantities of sand and gravel carried to the sea by glacial meltwaters were washed up and sorted by the waves. The most spectacular 'staircase' of such 'late-glacial' raised beaches occurs on Jura, where they occur at 20 levels.

A more accessible set may be seen at Glenacardoch Point, on the western coast of the Mull of Kintyre. The raised beaches were left high and dry whilst sea level dropped rapidly following the last glaciation.

Argyll is an important area for studying evidence of past changes in sea level, but the story that emerges is quite difficult to understand. For example, why has relative sea level clearly fallen by about 40 metres since the last glaciation when, during peak glacial conditions, the world's oceans were partly locked up in great continental ice sheets and sea level measured at the equator was actually about 120 metres below its level today? The explanation is that the enormous weight of ice caused the Scottish mainland to sag downwards by more than 120 metres. The land rapidly rebounded upwards after the ice sheet margin retreated inland, and it continues to rise very slowly today.

Those with a keen eye travelling around the district will discover that few of the raised beaches and platforms are actually horizontal. This is due to varying amounts of crustal rebound that has occurred following glaciation, and because the rate of rebound has decreased towards the present day. The features decline gently in elevation towards the southwest, the older ones are tilted the most, the youngest the least.

1
The indented coastline at Loch Craignish is influenced by the trend of the bedrock but shows flat platforms eroded during relatively recent times of higher sea level.

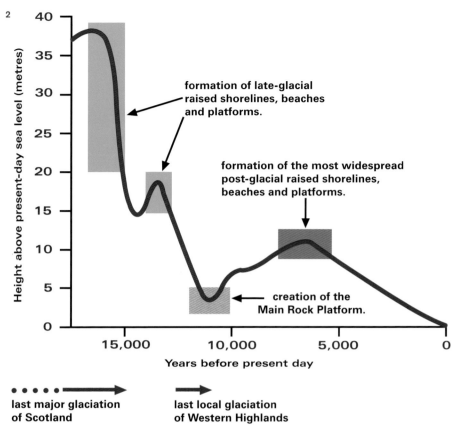

formation of late-glacial
raised shorelines, beaches
and platforms.

formation of the most widespread
post-glacial raised shorelines,
beaches and platforms.

creation of the
Main Rock Platform.

Height above present-day sea level (metres)

Years before present day

last major glaciation
of Scotland

last local glaciation
of Western Highlands

2
Changes in sea level in Knapdale
over the past 17,000 years.
3
Clach Tholl ('hole in the rock' in
Gaelic), southwest of Port Appin,
is a natural sea-arch associated
with the Main Rock Platform, which
formed by wave action 12,500 to
11,500 years ago.

Many abandoned coastal features appear to have been created during the short-lived return to glacial conditions that occurred between about 12,500 and 11,500 years ago, when sea level had dropped almost to its present level. Broad, rocky platforms and raised beaches backed by cliffs of this age almost encircle Lismore and are extensive on the islands of the Firth of Lorn, including Kerrera, Seil, Luing and Scarba. These flattish features of the so-called 'Main Rock Platform' provide relatively easy access on foot to many stretches of quite splendid coastal scenery, especially when primroses, flags and kingcups are flowering in the spring. Caves are quite common, especially in the limestone cliffs of Lismore. Elsewhere the platforms are associated with abandoned sea stacks, such as the Dog Stone immediately to the north of the promenade at Oban, and natural arches, such as below Gylen Castle on South Kerrera and, most notably, Clach Tholl, southwest of Port Appin.

3
Raised beach ridges at Rubh a'Mhail on the north coast of Islay.
4
A post-glacial raised beach on the south coast of Kerrera provides good pasture, nestling beside rocks of the Main Rock Platform (mid-distance) with higher, late-glacial, shelving wave-cut benches to the right.

Sea level dropped relative to the land for several thousand years following the creation of the Main Rock Platform, when Argyll was rebounding faster than the seas of the world were rising. New islands would have emerged as the sea withdrew, others would have been reunited with the mainland. However, relative sea level then rose again sharply, locally reaching a peak of about 10–12 metres above modern day sea level between 7,000 and 6,000 years ago. This 'high-stand' coincided with the final melting of ice sheets in North America and Scandinavia.

A distinct set of 'post-glacial' raised beaches and clifflines were created at this time. Several lower shorelines were formed subsequently, whilst sea level fell towards its present level. Exceptionally, as many as 31 unvegetated post-glacial raised beach ridges form a staircase that descends 12 metres to the present beach in southwest Jura. The shingle forming most post-glacial raised beaches is generally very well rounded as a result of being ground and polished by beach processes over many thousands of years.

5
The Dog Stone at Oban is an undercut, raised sea stack carved out of conglomerate. According to Gaelic legend, the giant Fingal tethered his dog, Bran, here whilst he went hunting in the Hebrides.

The Coast

The form of the much-indented coastline of the district is largely governed by the durability and structure of the underlying rocks, particularly in Knapdale. The natural southwesterly 'grain' of the landscape has been considerably enhanced by the passage of ice. Indeed, were it not for glacial erosion there would be far fewer islands than there are today. The coastline appears to change little in a human lifetime. However, the distribution of land and sea has clearly changed considerably since the last glaciation as a result of sea-level fluctuations. For example, the Rhinns of Islay were a separate island only a few thousand years ago, as was Kintyre, and only a slight rise in sea level would drown the low-tide connection between Colonsay and Oronsay. Loch Etive is a sea loch, but at every tide, water has to race over the Falls of Lora at the entrance to the loch. A further drop in sea level would disconnect the loch from the sea at the falls, turning it into a freshwater loch again. Our familiar map of this part of Scotland is just a snapshot in time.

1

2

Most of the coast is rocky, particularly stretches that are exposed to the full force of westerly gales, such as on the Rhinns of Islay and Colonsay. Sandy beaches favoured by holidaymakers nestle in sheltered bays. Mud flats and salt marshes have formed between the tidelines at the heads of sea lochs, providing important habitats for shellfish and flocks of wading birds. The intricate coastline and numerous islands are best examined by boat, but even the most experienced mariners must be aware of the strong tidal currents that regularly rip through narrow sounds, as at the 'Bridge over the Atlantic' to Seil. Tidal races are common because water is constricted within tapering inlets, like the Sound of Jura. In this particular case the water is forced through the Gulf of Corryvreckan, between Jura and Scarba, creating a notorious and particularly awesome whirlpool.

1
The so-called 'Bridge over the Atlantic' connects the island of Seil to the mainland of Argyll. It spans a narrow channel with a vigorous tidal race.
2
The Falls of Lora at Connel, where Loch Etive flows into the Firth of Lorn.
3
The whirlpool in the Gulf of Corryvreckan.

3

4
Machair flowers.
5
Daisies and silverweed are flowers often found growing on the machair.
6
Machair, Oronsay.

The Landscape Today

Modification of the landscape of coastal Argyll by Man has been going on since the Iron Age. In addition to the numerous fortifications, burial mounds and settlements, the progressive clearing of the natural forest for agriculture, fuel and timber has resulted in undoubtedly the greatest single change since the last Ice Age. This part of the Highlands does contain some of the largest remaining native oak woods in Britain, but it also includes wide expanses of commercial conifer plantations. Peat cutting has left its mark, particularly the large-scale commercial workings such as those on Islay that supply the distilling industry and give the Islay malt whiskies their distinctive taste and 'nose'.

Modern communications are very much influenced by the geology. On the peninsulas of the mainland most of the main roads follow the coast, taking full advantage of the almost continuous raised rock platforms and beaches. The Crinan Canal likewise follows a raised beach that cuts right across the peninsula along a line of weakness created initially by a fault in the bedrock. It therefore does not need to rise more than 20 metres above sea level. Campbeltown Airport, with one of the longest runways in Europe, is also sited on an extensive raised beach and alluvial deposits.

Probably the greatest impact of Man's industrial activity was the cutting down of forest in the 18th century to make charcoal to fuel iron furnaces locally at Bonawe and Furnace, but also farther afield in central Scotland.

The old slate quarries on the islands of Luing and Seil have largely been assimilated back into the landscape. However, the large quarries at Easdale that have been flooded by the sea are an enduring feature and are now part of a tourist attraction, firmly rooted in the geological heritage. Modern quarries in granitic rocks such as those at Bonawe and Furnace are less well concealed from view.

1
The flooded slate quarries on Easdale island are a significant artificial landscape feature that now form part of a visitor attraction.

2
The Crinan Canal follows a raised beach that cuts right across the Kintyre peninsula, a relic of when sea level was higher than today.

3
Quarries for hard-rock aggregate, like this one in fine-grained granitic rocks at Furnace, are less attractive man-made landscape features that are directly related to the bedrock geology.

4

5

Power generation has had a variable effect upon the landscape of this region, which can justifiably boast one of the least obtrusive power stations in Britain. The dam and upper reservoir of the Cruachan pump-storage scheme blend well into the slopes of the mountain, but the generator and all other installations are deep underground in huge self-supporting caverns that have been excavated out of the granite of the Etive Pluton.

4
The Cruachan dam and reservoir nestle into the landscape below Ben Cruachan and supply a power station that is completely underground.
5
Peat cutting, Islay.

The more recent proliferation of windfarms in the region has a much greater visual impact and, although they are an undeniable source of renewable energy and are particularly successful in small island communities, they are likely to remain controversial for the foreseeable future.

6
Windfarm near
Campbeltown.

Scottish Natural Heritage and the British Geological Survey

Scottish Natural Heritage is a government
body. Its aim is to help people enjoy
Scotland's natural heritage responsibly,
understand it more fully and use it wisely so
it can be sustained for future generations.

Scottish Natural Heritage
Great Glen House, Leachkin Road,
Inverness IV3 8NW
t: 01463 725000
e: enquiries@snh.gov.uk

**Scottish Natural Heritage
Dualchas Nàdair na h-Alba**
All of nature for all of Scotland
Nàdar air fad airson Alba air fad

The British Geological Survey maintains up-to-
date knowledge of the geology of the UK and
its continental shelf. It carries out surveys and
geological research.

The Scottish Office of BGS is sited in Edinburgh.
The office runs an advisory and information
service, a geological library and a well-stocked
geological bookshop.

British Geological Survey
Murchison House
West Mains Road
Edinburgh EH9 3LA
t : 0131 667 1000
f : 0131 668 2683

**British
Geological Survey**
NATURAL ENVIRONMENT RESEARCH COUNCIL

Also in the Landscape Fashioned by Geology series...

Arran and the Clyde Islands
David McAdam & Steve Robertson
ISBN 1 85397 287 8
Pbk 24pp £3.00

Ben Nevis and Glencoe
David Stephenson & Kathryn Goodenough
ISBN 1 85397 506 6
Pbk 44pp £4.95

Cairngorms
John Gordon, Rachel Wignall, Ness Brazier,
& Patricia Bruneau
ISBN 1 85397 455 2
Pbk 52pp £4.95

East Lothian and the Borders
David McAdam & Phil Stone
ISBN 1 85397 242 8
Pbk 26pp £3.00

Edinburgh and West Lothian
David McAdam
ISBN 1 85397 327 0
Pbk 44pp £4.95

Fife and Tayside
Mike Browne, Alan McKirdy & David McAdam
ISBN 1 85397 110 3
Pbk 36pp £3.95

Glasgow and Ayrshire
Colin MacFadyen & John Gordon
ISBN 1 85397 451 X
Pbk 52pp £4.95

Glen Roy
Douglas Peacock, John Gordon & Frank May
ISBN 1 85397 360 2
Pbk 36pp £4.95

Loch Lomond to Stirling
Mike Browne & John Mendum
ISBN 1 85397 119 7
Pbk 26pp £2.00

Mull and Iona
David Stephenson
ISBN 1 85397 423 4
Pbk 44pp £4.95

Northeast Scotland
Jon Merritt & Graham Leslie
ISBN 978 1 85397 521 9
Pbk 76pp Price £7.95

Northwest Highlands
John Mendum, Jon Merritt & Alan McKirdy
ISBN 1 85397 139 1
Pbk 52pp £6.95

Orkney and Shetland
Alan McKirdy
ISBN 978 1 85397 602 5
Pbk 68pp £7.95

The Outer Hebrides
Kathryn Goodenough & Jon Merritt
ISBN 1 978185397 507 3
Pbk 44pp £4.95

Rum and the Small Isles
Kathryn Goodenough & Tom Bradwell
ISBN 1 85397 370 2
Pbk 48pp £5.95

Scotland: the creation of its natural landscape
Alan McKirdy & Roger Crofts
ISBN 1 85397 004 2
Pbk 64pp £7.50

Skye
David Stephenson & Jon Merritt
ISBN 1 85397 026 3
Pbk 24pp £3.95

Southwest Scotland
Andrew McMillan & Phil Stone
ISBN 978 1 85397 520 2
Pbk 48pp £4.95

Series Editor: Alan McKirdy (SNH)
Other books soon to be produced in the series
include: Moray & Caithness

To order these and other publications, visit: www.snh.gov.uk/pubs